Why Am I Broke?

Unraveling the Mysteries of Financial Struggle

Vincent Angel

Dedication:

This book is dedicated to every individual who embodies the enduring qualities of patience and perseverance in the face of life's challenges. To those who refuse to be deterred by setbacks and obstacles, but instead press on with unwavering determination and faith in their abilities.

As we navigate the turbulent waters of our personal and entrepreneurial journeys, may this book serve as a guiding light, illuminating the path ahead and offering insights to help us navigate the complexities of success and failure. In times of doubt and uncertainty, may it remind us that every trial and tribulation is but a stepping stone on the road to achievement.

With each turn of the page, let us reaffirm our commitment to hard work, resilience, and the belief that with time and effort, our labor will yield fruit. Here's to the dreamers, the doers, and the believers, to those who dare to chase their dreams and refuse to be bound by the limitations of the present.

May this book inspire you to reach for the stars, to persevere in the face of adversity, and to never lose sight of the limitless potential that lies within you.

With hope and determination,

Vincent Angel

"Why Am I Broke? Unraveling the Mysteries of Financial Struggle" by Vincent Angel

Copyright © 2024 by Vincent Angel

All rights reserved. No part of this publication may be reproduced, distributed, or transmitted in any form or by any means, including photocopying, recording, or other electronic or mechanical methods, without the prior written permission of the publisher, except in the case of brief quotations embodied in critical reviews and certain other non-commercial uses permitted by copyright law.

For permission requests, write to the publisher, at the email address: vincentangelbooks@yahoo.com

Table of Contents

Introduction: The puzzle of poverty 4

Chapter 1. From Rags to Riches: Inspiring Tales of Triumph 9

The Stories of Visionaries: Entrepreneurs Who Transformed Challenges into Opportunities 9

Overcoming Adversity: Understanding the Struggles Faced by Self-Made Entrepreneurs 10

1.2 Lessons from the Trenches: Key Themes in Entrepreneurial Journeys 10

1.3 Embracing Failure: The Path to Success is Paved with Setbacks 12

1.4 From Basement Beginnings to Billion-Dollar Empires 14

1.5 The Impact Beyond Wealth: Contributions to Society and Legacy Building 16

Chapter 2: Breaking the Chains of Generational Poverty 18

Chapter 3: The Mindset of Success 23

Chapter 4: Navigating Economic Barriers: Not Your Average Treasure Hunt 31

Chapter 5: Harnessing the Power of Education: Building Bridges to Opportunity 34

Chapter 6: Embracing Entrepreneurship: Forging Paths to Economic Independence 38

Chapter 7: Investing in Yourself: The Journey Within 42

Chapter 8: Building Strong Communities: The Foundation of Social Prosperity 46

Chapter 9: Harnessing Environmental Awareness to Break the Cycle of Poverty..53

Chapter 10: The Journey to Financial Freedom: Empowering Yourself for Economic Independence 57

Chapter 11: Final Reflections..61

About Me 63

Introduction: The puzzle of poverty

"Poverty was the greatest motivating factor in my life" ... Jimmy Dean

Encouragement and motivation cannot solely rely on words. It must come from within, deep in thought. This leads me to ask myself, and you, my reader, the rhetorical question: "Why am I poor?" In a world full of opportunities, it is easy to feel left behind. However, we cannot find a solution through self-pity or resentment.

I recently watched again Sinead O'Connor's popular song "Nothing compares 2 U" and was amazed to learn that it was originally written by Prince for his band "The Family", but it did not become a hit until Sinead released it in her second album. Despite Prince's fame, it was Sinead's version that propelled the song to international success, topping charts in multiple countries and earning platinum and gold certifications. This serves as a reminder that sometimes it takes the right person to bring a great piece of art to its full potential. In the United States, it spent four weeks at the top of the Billboard Hot 100; in addition, it was number one on the Billboard Alternative Songs chart.

Many times, we seek that breakthrough, that will just propel our careers or business and this book will illustrate how we can create a pathway.

Many of the wealthiest people in the world today began their journey from humble beginnings. It is important to understand that not everyone receives a head start in life, which begs the question: what is stopping you from achieving your goals?

Whether you are starting out in a small town or a big city, it is important to remember that success is not determined by where you start, but by the actions you take to move forward.

I recently read about famous individuals who began from nothing and made it to the top. Jeff Bezos, the founder of Amazon, started his business in his garage. Steve Jobs and Steve Wozniak started Apple in Jobs' parents' garage. Mark Zuckerberg started Facebook in his Harvard dorm room. Larry Page and Sergey Brin, the founders of Google, started their company in a garage as well. These individuals were able to create something from nothing and build it into a successful business.

Although, the reality of life may have made our dreams more humble, and having a garage may not be common in every part of the world. Nevertheless, the most important thing to learn from their stories is to have a vision or an idea, believe in it, and find yourself among those who share your dream and are ready to offer mental support.

Surrounding yourself with the right people is crucial to achieving your goals. The truth is, you cannot move forward if you are surrounded by the wrong company. It is good to have friends who make you see the realities of life, but it is wrong to always be around people who lack drive and do not contribute to your goals.

I have studied why many people despised the Jews, especially in Europe when the European society was predominantly Christian. The fact is, during those times, it was un-Christian to loan money and ask for interest. The Jews had no problem with it. Looking at the Rothschild dynasty at that time, this is how they became rich. Today, we have banks and finance houses. That was foresight!

When you see people like Gates, Jobs, Bezos, and others, remember that they thought of something before its time, which is extraordinary. Their success did not come overnight, but it was the result of hard work, dedication, and perseverance.

Let's make things simple by looking at the people around us who we perceive as lucky, such as the man who owns a grocery store and can send his kids to school, the man who has been a taxi driver but has led a happy life, the woman who has a hairdressing salon and has excelled in her business, or the man or woman who has worked in an organized sector for years and has always provided for their family. These individuals may not be famous or have a lot of money, but they have found success in their own way.

Poverty is often a mindset. Just because you are moving slowly and the road seems long does not mean you have failed. The road to success is not always easy, and it requires hard work, dedication, and perseverance. With the right mindset and support, you can achieve your goals and find success in your own way.

Chapter 1. From Rags to Riches: Inspiring Tales of Triumph

The Stories of Visionaries: Entrepreneurs Who Transformed Challenges into Opportunities

One such visionary is Oprah Winfrey, who rose from poverty in rural Mississippi to become one of the most influential media moguls in the world. Despite facing adversity throughout her childhood, including poverty and abuse, Winfrey persevered, leveraging her innate talent for communication to build an empire that includes television networks, magazines, and philanthropic endeavours.

Overcoming Adversity: Understanding the Struggles Faced by Self-Made Entrepreneurs

Another inspiring example is Jack Ma, the founder of Alibaba Group. Ma faced numerous rejections and setbacks early in his career, including being rejected from Harvard ten times and being turned down for numerous jobs. Despite these challenges, Ma persisted, eventually founding Alibaba in his apartment in Hangzhou, China. Today, Alibaba is one of the world's largest e-commerce companies, and Ma is one of the richest individuals in China.

1.2 Lessons from the Trenches: Key Themes in Entrepreneurial Journeys

Persistence Pays Off: Examining the Role of Grit and Determination

Elon Musk, the founder of SpaceX and Tesla, exemplifies the importance of persistence in entrepreneurship. Musk faced numerous setbacks and near-bankruptcy with both companies but remained undeterred in his pursuit of his vision for the future of space exploration and sustainable transportation.

Risk and Reward: Navigating Uncertainty in Pursuit of Success

Richard Branson, the founder of the Virgin Group, is known for his willingness to take risks in pursuit of innovation. From starting a record store as a teenager to launching Virgin Galactic, Branson has always embraced uncertainty, seeing it as an opportunity rather than a deterrent. His boldness has paid off, with Virgin Group encompassing over four hundred companies in various industries.

1.3 Embracing Failure: The Path to Success is Paved with Setbacks

from How of Entrepreneurs

Learning Mistakes: Failures Shape the Trajectory

J.K. Rowling, the author of the Harry Potter series, faced numerous rejections from publishers before finally finding success. Rowling has spoken openly about the role failure played in her journey, emphasizing the importance of resilience and perseverance in the face of adversity.

Resilience and Adaptability: Strategies for Bouncing Back Stronger

Howard Schultz, the former CEO of Starbucks, was fired from his job at a housewares company before joining Starbucks as a marketing director. Schultz went on to transform Starbucks from a small chain of coffee shops into a global powerhouse, demonstrating the power of resilience and adaptability in the face of setbacks.

These real-life examples illustrate the themes of perseverance, risk-taking, learning from failure, and resilience that are central to the entrepreneurial journey.

1.4 From Basement Beginnings to Billion-Dollar Empires

The Myth of the Overnight Success: Understanding the Long Road to Achievement

One notable example is Jeff Bezos, who famously started Amazon in his garage in Bellevue, Washington. Bezos initially faced scepticism and doubts from investors, but through his relentless focus on customer satisfaction and long-term vision, Amazon grew from an online bookstore into one of the world's largest e-commerce platforms. Bezos' journey underscores the importance of perseverance and patience in building a successful business.

Scaling the Heights: How Self-Made Entrepreneurs Built Their Companies from the Ground Up

Another inspiring example is Sara Blakely, the founder of Spanx. Blakely started her company with just $5,000 and operated it out of her apartment. Through innovative product design and savvy marketing, Blakely grew Spanx into a billion-dollar business, revolutionizing the shapewear industry in the process. Blakely's story demonstrates the power of creativity and resourcefulness in building a successful brand from humble beginnings.

1.5 The Impact Beyond Wealth: Contributions to Society and Legacy Building

Philanthropy and Social Responsibility: Giving Back to Communities

One exemplary philanthropist is Bill Gates, the co-founder of Microsoft. After stepping down as CEO of Microsoft, Gates focused his efforts on philanthropy through the Bill & Melinda Gates Foundation. The foundation works to improve global health, education, and access to information technology, with a particular focus on addressing poverty and inequality. Gates' commitment to giving back highlights the importance of using wealth and influence to make a positive impact on society.

Inspiring the Next Generation: The Ripple Effect of Entrepreneurial Success

Elon Musk, in addition to his groundbreaking work with SpaceX and Tesla, is known for his efforts to inspire and mentor the next generation of entrepreneurs. Musk has spoken about the importance of pursuing ambitious goals and pushing the boundaries of innovation, encouraging others to follow their passions and strive for greatness. Musk's advocacy for entrepreneurship serves as a catalyst for future generations to pursue their dreams and make a difference in the world.

These examples illustrate how self-made entrepreneurs have not only achieved remarkable success but have also made significant contributions to society and inspired others to follow in their footsteps. From humble beginnings in basements and garages to billion-dollar empires and philanthropic endeavours, their stories serve as a testament to the transformative power of entrepreneurship.

Chapter 2: Breaking the Chains of Generational Poverty

When exploring the topic of generational poverty, it is crucial to understand its profound impact on individuals, families, and communities. Generational poverty refers to a cycle that persists across multiple generations within a family. This cycle is often perpetuated by a combination of systemic barriers, limited access to resources, and social inequalities. Breaking free from the chains of generational poverty requires a concerted effort to address its root causes and empower individuals to create a brighter future for themselves and their families.

Many people have taken steps to change this family narrative by leaving their comfort zones. This triggers migration to their country's city centers and other countries, no matter how big or small. This has worked for some, but for others, the tale is different.

It is important to acknowledge that breaking the cycle of generational poverty is a complex and challenging task that requires a multifaceted approach. This involves not only providing access to education and job opportunities but also addressing the systemic barriers and social inequalities that perpetuate poverty. Additionally, it requires a shift in societal attitudes towards poverty and a recognition of the inherent dignity and worth of all individuals. By working together and supporting one another, we can create a more just and equitable society where everyone can thrive.

Understanding the Impact of Family Background:

Family background plays a significant role in shaping an individual's socioeconomic trajectory. Growing up in poverty can have far-reaching effects on a person's education, employment opportunities, and overall well-being. Children born into poverty are more likely to experience adverse childhood experiences, such as food insecurity, inadequate housing, and limited access to healthcare. These early life experiences can have lasting effects on physical and mental health, as well as academic achievement.

Moreover, the intergenerational transmission of poverty perpetuates a cycle of disadvantage, as children from low-income families often face barriers to accessing quality education and breaking into higher-paying careers. Without adequate support and resources, they may struggle to overcome these obstacles and achieve economic stability, thus perpetuating the cycle for future generations.

Strategies for Breaking Generational Cycles:
Breaking the cycle of generational poverty requires a multi-faceted approach that addresses both individual and systemic barriers. Education plays a critical role in empowering individuals to overcome poverty and build a better future. By investing in early childhood education, expanding access to quality K-12 schooling (mostly in the United States), and providing support for higher education and vocational training, we can equip individuals with the skills and knowledge needed to succeed in today's economy.

Countries where government has failed its citizens towards affordable education, individuals must help themselves with the ultimate sacrifice to get educated no matter how small it might seem. Even getting data and learning courses on YouTube will help stimulate the mind towards your goals. Your focus should be accumulation of knowledge no matter the source.

Additionally, interventions that address the social determinants of health, such as affordable housing, access to healthcare, and nutritious food, can help mitigate the adverse effects of poverty on individuals and families. Programs that provide wraparound services, such as job training, financial literacy education, and mental health support, can also be effective in breaking the cycle of poverty by addressing the underlying factors that contribute to economic insecurity.

Furthermore, efforts to promote economic mobility and reduce income inequality are essential for creating a more equitable society. This includes policies that raise the minimum wage, expand access to affordable childcare, and provide support for working families, such as the Earned Income Tax Credit and child tax credits. By addressing the structural barriers that perpetuate poverty, we can create pathways to opportunity for all members of society.

In conclusion, breaking the chains of generational poverty is a complex and challenging endeavour, but it is essential for building a more just and equitable society. By addressing the root causes of poverty, investing in education and economic opportunity, and promoting policies that support working families, we can create a future where every individual can thrive, regardless of their family background. Through collective action and commitment to social change, we can break the cycle of poverty and build a brighter future for generations to come.

Chapter 3: The Mindset of Success

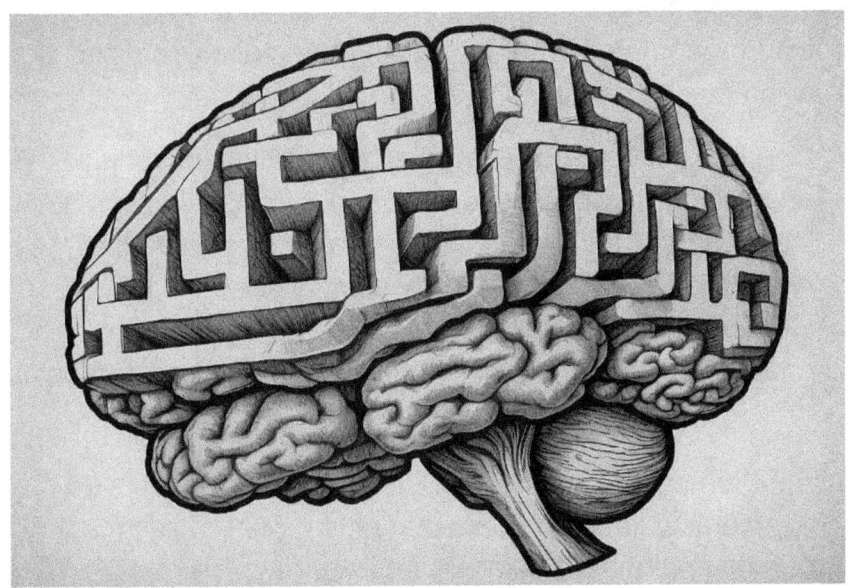

The mindset of success is a powerful force that shapes our attitudes, beliefs, and behaviours towards achieving our goals. It encompasses a combination of optimism, resilience, determination, and a growth mindset that allows individuals to overcome challenges and pursue their aspirations with confidence and persistence. In this chapter, we will explore the principles of success mindset and how cultivating it can empower individuals to realize their full potential and achieve extraordinary results in their personal and professional lives.

Cultivating a Prosperity Mindset:

At the core of the success mindset is a belief in abundance and possibility. A prosperity mindset is characterized by optimism, gratitude, and a focus on opportunities rather than limitations. Instead of dwelling on past failures or setbacks, individuals with a prosperity mindset maintain a positive outlook and actively seek out solutions to challenges. They view obstacles as temporary setbacks rather than insurmountable barriers, and they approach every situation with a sense of curiosity and openness to learning.

One key aspect of cultivating a prosperity mindset is practicing gratitude. By focusing on the positive aspects of life and expressing gratitude for the blessings we have, we can shift our perspective from scarcity to abundance. Gratitude fosters resilience and emotional well-being, enabling us to navigate adversity with grace and perspective.

Overcoming Limiting Beliefs:

Another important aspect of the success mindset is overcoming limiting beliefs that hold us back from reaching our full potential. Limiting beliefs are negative or self-defeating thoughts that undermine our confidence and hinder our progress towards our goals. These beliefs often stem from past experiences, societal conditioning, or fear of failure.

Many beliefs that limit us might be cultural or religious, which in some cases has been interpreted by individuals who have deviated from the original doctrines of worship. Today, you find worshippers quoting their pastors instead of the Bible or their imams instead of the Quran.

In many countries, the prevalence of a political affinity mindset poses a significant challenge. This mindset involves individuals aligning themselves with a particular political group without fully understanding how government policies impact their circumstances. As a result, these individuals may overlook certain root causes of failure in their entrepreneurial endeavours.

The poor in many societies tend to be misled by their hearts and not their heads, voting based on ethnicity or religious affiliation, unlike the rich who probably support a candidate for policies or power.

To break free from the political affinity mindset and its potential negative impact on entrepreneurial endeavours', individuals can take several steps:

1. Educate Yourself: Individuals should educate themselves about the broader political and economic landscape, including understanding how government policies directly affect their business environment and opportunities.

2. Critical Thinking: Encourage critical thinking and independent analysis of political affiliations and policies. Instead of blindly following a particular political group, individuals should assess the actual impact of policies on their lives and businesses.

3. Diversify Information Sources: Seek out diverse sources of information and perspectives to gain a more comprehensive understanding of political issues and their implications. This helps to avoid echo chambers and confirmation bias.

4. Focus on Business Fundamentals: Instead of relying solely on political connections or affiliations, prioritize building a solid foundation for the business based on sound principles of entrepreneurship, including market research, fiscal management, and customer satisfaction.

5. Community Engagement: Engage with local communities and business networks to share knowledge, experiences,

and resources. Collaborating with like-minded individuals can provide support and guidance outside of political affiliations.

6. Advocacy and Civic Engagement: Advocate for policies and reforms that support a conducive business environment and economic development, regardless of political alignment. Civic engagement can empower individuals to influence positive change and create opportunities for entrepreneurship.

To overcome limiting beliefs, it is essential to challenge and reframe them with more empowering and constructive beliefs. This process involves self-awareness, introspection, and a willingness to confront our inner fears and insecurities. By replacing negative self-talk with positive affirmations and reframing challenges as opportunities for growth, we can transform our mindset and unlock our true potential.

Practical Strategies for Cultivating a Success Mindset:

1. Set Clear Goals: Define your vision for success and set specific, achievable goals that align with your values and aspirations.

2. Develop Resilience: Embrace failure as a natural part of the learning process and use setbacks as opportunities for growth and self-improvement.

3. Practice Positive Self-Talk: Monitor your inner dialogue and replace negative thoughts with affirmations and encouragement.

4. Seek Inspiration: Surround yourself with positive influences, such as mentors, role models, and supportive peers, who inspire and motivate you to pursue your dreams.

5. Act: Break down your goals into actionable steps and take consistent, deliberate action towards their achievement.

The mindset of success is an essential ingredient in the recipe for a fulfilling and prosperous life. It is a powerful catalyst for personal and professional growth, enabling individuals to surpass their limitations, seize opportunities, and achieve their dreams.

Cultivating a prosperity mindset involves developing a positive attitude towards our capabilities and potential. It requires us to identify and overcome limiting beliefs that may be holding us back from reaching our goals. This can be challenging, as limiting beliefs often stem from past experiences, societal norms, or self-doubt. However, by acknowledging and challenging these beliefs, we can unlock our full potential and create a life of purpose, fulfillment, and abundance.

Adopting practical strategies for success is another critical aspect of cultivating a prosperity mindset. This may involve setting achievable goals, creating a plan of action, and taking consistent steps towards achieving those goals. It may also involve seeking out mentors, learning new skills, and embracing a growth mindset that encourages us to view challenges as opportunities for growth. As we embrace the principles of the success mindset, we empower ourselves to create positive change in our lives and make a meaningful impact on the world around us. We become more resilient, adaptable, and optimistic, and we are better able to navigate the ups and downs of life with grace and ease.

Chapter 4: Navigating Economic Barriers: Not Your Average Treasure Hunt

Ahoy, mateys! Welcome aboard as we set sail on the turbulent seas of economic barriers. In this chapter, we will be navigating through the treacherous waters of financial challenges, grappling with the elusive beasts of systemic inequality, and unearthing the hidden treasures of opportunity amidst the stormy seas of adversity. So, batten down the hatches and hoist the sails as we embark on this daring adventure!

Analyzing Systemic Challenges:

As we chart our course through the murky depths of economic barriers, it is crucial to recognize the formidable foes that stand in our way. From the towering cliffs of income inequality to the swirling whirlpools of institutional discrimination, these systemic challenges can seem insurmountable to even the most intrepid adventurers. But fear not, for with a keen eye and a sturdy ship, we can navigate these perilous waters and emerge victorious on the other side.

One of the most notorious pirates of economic inequality is the nefarious wealth gap, a monstrous leviathan that looms large over the horizon. This ravenous beast hoards treasure plundered from the coffers of the poor, leaving them stranded on desert islands of poverty while the affluent sail their gilded ships across the seas of prosperity. But fear not, for with a cleverly crafted map of economic empowerment, we can outmanoeuvre this rapacious foe and claim our rightful share of the bounty.

Tactics for Overcoming Economic Hurdles:

Now that we have identified our adversaries, it is time to plot our course to victory. But beware, for the waters ahead are teeming with obstacles and challenges aplenty. From the jagged reefs of unemployment to the treacherous shoals of debt, there are countless hazards that threaten to dash our hopes upon the rocks of despair. But fear not, for with a hearty crew of allies and a trusty compass of financial literacy, we can navigate these perilous waters and chart a course to financial freedom.

One invaluable tool in our arsenal is the mighty ship of entrepreneurship, a sturdy vessel that can weather even the fiercest storms of economic uncertainty. With a bold captain at the helm and a crew of intrepid sailors by our side, we can set sail for uncharted waters and stake our claim to riches untold. But beware, for the seas of entrepreneurship are not for the faint of heart. From the tempestuous squalls of market competition to the lurking sea monsters of regulatory red tape, there are dangers aplenty that threaten to sink our ship. But fear not, for with courage, cunning, and a dash of good fortune, we can navigate these treacherous waters and emerge victorious in the end.

As our adventure draws to a close and we prepare to weigh anchor once more, let us reflect on the lessons we have learned and the treasures we have uncovered along the way. Though the seas of economic barriers may be rough and unforgiving, with determination, resilience, and a hearty sense of humour, we can navigate them with confidence and emerge stronger on the other side. So, hoist the Jolly Roger of opportunity high and set course for the horizon, for the greatest treasures await those brave enough to seek them!

Chapter 5: Harnessing the Power of Education: Building Bridges to Opportunity

Education stands as the beacon of hope, illuminating the path towards a brighter future. In this chapter, we embark on a journey to explore the transformative power of education in breaking down barriers and opening doors to opportunity. From the halls of academia to the digital classrooms of the future, let us delve deep into the realms of learning and discover the keys to unlocking our full potential.

The Role of Education in Economic Mobility:

Education serves as the great equalizer, offering individuals from all walks of life the chance to rise above their circumstances and achieve economic mobility. By providing access to knowledge, skills, and opportunities, education empowers individuals to break free from the chains of poverty and chart their own course towards success. Whether through formal schooling, vocational training, or lifelong learning initiatives, education lays the foundation for a more equitable and prosperous society.

Accessing Education in Modern Society:

Despite its importance, access to quality education remains a challenge for many individuals, particularly those from marginalized communities. Barriers such as socioeconomic status, geographical location, and systemic inequalities often prevent individuals from accessing the educational resources they need to succeed. In today's digital age, however,

technology has emerged as a powerful tool for expanding access to education and bridging the gap between learners and resources. Online courses, virtual classrooms, and educational apps offer new pathways to learning, allowing individuals to access educational content anytime, anywhere.

Strategies for Empowering Learners:

Empowering learners to seize the opportunities afforded by education requires a multifaceted approach that addresses both systemic barriers and individual needs. At the systemic level, policymakers must prioritize investment in education, ensuring that schools are adequately funded, teachers are supported, and resources are equitably distributed. Additionally, efforts to promote diversity, equity, and inclusion in educational settings are essential for creating a learning environment where all students feel valued and supported.

On an individual level, fostering a culture of lifelong learning is key to empowering learners to adapt and thrive in an ever-changing world. By instilling a growth mindset and a love of learning from an early age, educators and parents can equip students with the tools they need to succeed both inside and outside the classroom. Additionally, providing support services such as tutoring, mentorship, and career counselling can help learners overcome obstacles and achieve their academic and professional goals.

As we conclude our exploration of the power of education, let us reaffirm our commitment to building a world where every individual has the opportunity to learn, grow, and succeed. By investing in education and empowering learners to reach their full potential, we can break down barriers, foster economic mobility, and create a more equitable and prosperous society for all. So let us continue to champion the transformative power of education and work together to build a brighter future for generations to come.

Chapter 6: Embracing Entrepreneurship: Forging Paths to Economic Independence

Welcome to the thrilling realm of entrepreneurship, where dreams take flight and innovation knows no bounds. In this chapter, we embark on an exhilarating journey to explore the transformative power of entrepreneurship in driving economic growth, fostering innovation, and empowering individuals to chart their own destinies. From the humble beginnings of startups to the soaring heights of global enterprises, let us delve deep into the world of entrepreneurship and discover the keys to building a more prosperous future.

Entrepreneurial Opportunities in the Digital Age:
In today's interconnected world, the digital landscape has opened up a wealth of opportunities for aspiring entrepreneurs. From e-commerce platforms to social media marketing, technology has revolutionized the way businesses

operate and connect with customers. With the click of a button, entrepreneurs can launch their own businesses, reach global markets, and scale their ventures with unprecedented speed and efficiency. The barriers to entry have never been lower, making entrepreneurship more accessible and achievable than ever before.

Building Wealth through Innovation:

At the heart of entrepreneurship lies the spirit of innovation, driving forward progress and propelling society towards new frontiers. Entrepreneurs are the trailblazers, the risk-takers, and the visionaries who dare to challenge the status quo and push the boundaries of what is possible. Whether through groundbreaking inventions, disruptive business models, or novel solutions to pressing challenges, entrepreneurs are the engine of economic growth and the architects of a brighter future.

Take, for example, Elon Musk, the visionary founder of SpaceX, Tesla, and numerous other ventures. Musk's relentless pursuit of innovation has revolutionized industries ranging from space exploration to renewable energy, demonstrating the transformative power of entrepreneurship to drive positive change on a global scale.

Navigating the Entrepreneurial Landscape:

While entrepreneurship offers boundless opportunities, it also presents its fair share of challenges and uncertainties. From navigating regulatory hurdles to securing funding and managing cash flow, entrepreneurs must navigate a complex landscape fraught with pitfalls and obstacles. Yet, it is precisely these challenges that fuel the entrepreneurial spirit, inspiring individuals to persevere in the face of adversity and emerge stronger and more resilient than ever before.

To succeed as an entrepreneur, one must cultivate a diverse skill set that encompasses creativity, adaptability, resilience, and strategic thinking. It requires the ability to identify opportunities, assess risks, and pivot quickly in response to changing market dynamics. Moreover, it requires a willingness to embrace failure as an integral part of the learning process, recognizing that every setback is an opportunity for growth and improvement.

Let us celebrate the spirit of innovation and enterprise that drives progress and prosperity around the world. By embracing entrepreneurship and empowering individuals to pursue their dreams, we can unlock new opportunities, unleash human potential, and build a more vibrant and resilient economy for future generations. So let us continue to champion the entrepreneurial spirit and work together to create a world where every individual can succeed and thrive.

Chapter 7: Investing in Yourself: The Journey Within

In the quiet solitude of dawn, as the first light breaks over the horizon, a journey of self-discovery begins. In the heart of every individual lies a vast landscape waiting to be explored, filled with untapped potential, hidden treasures, and uncharted territories of the soul. Welcome to the realm of self-investment, where the greatest adventure of all unfolds the journey within.

As our protagonist sets out on this quest, they find themselves standing at the crossroads of possibility, surrounded by the whispers of dreams yet to be realized and the echoes of past triumphs and tribulations. In the distance, a beacon of light beckons, promising hope and transformation for those brave enough to heed its call.

But this journey is not for the faint of heart, for the path ahead is fraught with challenges and obstacles that test the limits of courage and resilience. From the tangled thickets of self-doubt to the stormy seas of uncertainty, our protagonists must navigate a labyrinth of emotions and experiences as they seek to uncover the truths that lie hidden within.

Along the way, they encounter fellow travellers' kindred spirits who share in the quest for self-discovery and personal growth. Together, they form a community of seekers, bound by a common purpose and a shared commitment to unlocking their fullest potential.

As our protagonist delves deeper into the recesses of their being, they discover a wealth of resources waiting to be harnessed—a treasure trove of talents, passions, and aspirations just waiting to be unleashed. With each step forward, they gain new insights, acquire new skills, and forge new pathways towards a brighter and more fulfilling future.

But the journey of self-investment is not just about acquiring knowledge or mastering skills; it is also about embracing the journey itself the joys, the struggles, and everything in between. It is about learning to embrace the process of growth and transformation, trusting in the wisdom of the heart and the guidance of the soul.

As the sun sets on the horizon and the journey draws to a close, our protagonist emerges from the depths of their own being, forever changed by the experiences they have encountered along the way. With newfound clarity and purpose, they step boldly into the world, ready to embrace the adventure that lies ahead.

For in the end, the greatest investment we can ever make is in ourselves—in our dreams, our passions, and our potential to create a life filled with meaning, purpose, and fulfilment. And so, dear reader, I invite you to embark on your own journey of self-investment, knowing that the greatest adventure of all awaits within.

Chapter 8: Building Strong Communities: The Foundation of Social Prosperity

In the tapestry of human existence, communities serve as the warp and weft, weaving together the fabric of society. In this chapter, we embark on a profound exploration of the role of communities in fostering social prosperity and collective well-being. From the bustling city streets to the tranquil countryside, let us delve deep into the intricate web of human connections and discover the transformative power of community building.

The Essence of Community:

At its core, a community is more than just a collection of individuals living in close proximity—it is a living, breathing organism, bound together by shared values, experiences, and aspirations. It is a place where bonds are forged, friendships are nurtured, and support is freely given. In a world that often feels fragmented and disconnected, communities serve as oases of belonging and solidarity, offering refuge from the storms of life and a sense of belonging that is deeply rooted in the human spirit.

But what makes a community strong? Is it the physical infrastructure—the schools, parks, and libraries—that provide the foundation for collective life? Or is it the intangible qualities—the sense of belonging, the spirit of cooperation, the culture of inclusivity—that breathe life into the fabric of community?

Building Blocks of Community Strength:

To answer these questions, we must first examine the building blocks of community strength—the pillars upon which vibrant and resilient communities are built. At the heart of every strong community lies a sense of belonging—a feeling of being part of something greater than oneself. This sense of belonging fosters trust, empathy, and solidarity, creating a fertile ground for collaboration and collective action.

But belonging alone is not enough. Strong communities also require strong social networks—webs of relationships that connect individuals, families, and organizations in a tapestry of mutual support and shared responsibility. These networks serve as conduits for information, resources, and social capital, enabling communities to weather storms, overcome challenges, and seize opportunities for growth and renewal.

Moreover, strong communities are characterized by a culture of inclusivity and diversity—a recognition that every voice matters and every individual has a role to play in shaping the collective destiny. Inclusive communities celebrate differences, embrace diversity, and strive to create spaces where all members feel valued, respected, and empowered to contribute their unique gifts and talents.

Strategies for Community Building:

But how do we cultivate these qualities of belonging, social networks, and inclusivity within our communities? The answer lies in intentional and collaborative efforts to build and strengthen the social fabric that binds us together. This can take many forms, from grassroots organizing and civic engagement to community-based initiatives and collaborative partnerships.

One effective strategy is to invest in community infrastructure building parks, libraries, community centers, and other public spaces that serve as gathering places for residents of all ages and backgrounds. These spaces not only provide opportunities for recreation and leisure but also serve as hubs for social interaction, cultural exchange, and civic engagement.

Another strategy especially when there is no finance is to foster a culture of volunteerism and service a spirit of giving back to the community with your time. By mobilizing volunteers, organizing service projects, and promoting a culture of philanthropy, communities can harness the collective power of individuals and organizations to address pressing social challenges and improve the quality of life for all residents.

In exploration of community building, let us reflect on the profound impact that strong and resilient communities can have on the well-being and prosperity of society. By fostering a sense of belonging, nurturing social networks, and embracing inclusivity and diversity, communities can become powerful agents of positive change, creating a more equitable, just, and vibrant world for generations to come. So let us continue to invest in the strength and resilience of our communities, knowing that together, we can build a brighter future for all.

The following paragraphs provide a few examples of how communities have come together to foster resilience, growth, and prosperity.

1. Community Gardens and Urban Farms: In many urban areas, community gardens and urban farms have sprung up, bringing together residents to grow fresh produce, beautify neighbourhoods, and promote sustainability. For example, the Detroit Black Community Food Security Network operates

several urban farms in Detroit, Michigan, providing residents with access to healthy food and fostering community engagement and empowerment.

2. Community Centres and Hubs: Community centres and hubs serve as focal points for community activities, offering a wide range of programs and services for residents of all ages. For instance, the Queens Library in New York City serves as a vibrant community hub, providing not only books and resources but also hosting events, workshops, and classes that bring together residents from diverse backgrounds.

3. Volunteer Organizations and Service Projects: Volunteer organizations and service projects play a crucial role in community building by mobilizing individuals to address local needs and challenges. For example, Habitat for Humanity organizes volunteers to build affordable housing for low-income families, fostering a sense of camaraderie and solidarity among participants while making a tangible difference in the lives of others.

4. Cultural Festivals and Events: Cultural festivals and events celebrate diversity, promote cultural exchange, and strengthen community bonds. For instance, the Notting Hill Carnival in London, England, brings together people from various ethnic backgrounds to celebrate Caribbean culture through music, dance, and food, fostering a sense of unity and belonging among participants and spectators alike.

5. Online Communities and social media: In today's digital age, online communities and social media platforms provide opportunities for connection and collaboration, transcending

geographical boundaries. For example, online forums and groups dedicated to specific interests or causes allow individuals to share information, offer support, and organize collective action, fostering a sense of belonging and empowerment among participants.

These examples illustrate the diverse ways in which communities come together to build strength, resilience, and prosperity, demonstrating the transformative power of community building in enhancing the well-being of society.

Chapter 9: Harnessing Environmental Awareness to Break the Cycle of Poverty

In this pivotal chapter, we explore the symbiotic relationship between poverty and environmental degradation while providing actionable strategies for you to overcome these intertwined challenges and pave their path towards prosperity.

Understanding the Environmental Dimension of Poverty: The first step towards overcoming poverty's grip is understanding its multifaceted nature, including its environmental implications. Poverty often leads to resource exploitation and limited access to clean air, water, and land. Moreover, environmental degradation can exacerbate poverty by destroying livelihoods and increasing vulnerability to natural disasters. Recognizing this nexus empowers individuals to address both poverty and environmental issues simultaneously.

Empowering Personal and Community Action:

You can initiate change by taking proactive steps within your community. Simple actions like reducing waste, conserving energy, and advocating for sustainable practices can make a significant impact. By participating in community clean-up events, supporting local environmental initiatives, and raising awareness about environmental issues, individuals can mobilize collective action and effect positive change at the grassroots level.

Exploring Opportunities for Sustainable Livelihoods:
Breaking free from poverty requires exploring sustainable livelihood options that promote economic stability while minimizing environmental harm. You can explore opportunities in green industries such as renewable energy, organic farming, eco-tourism, and conservation efforts. By harnessing your skills and passions to create sustainable businesses and employment opportunities, individuals can uplift themselves and their communities while contributing to environmental conservation.

Building Resilience to Environmental Challenges:
As you embark on your journey out of poverty, it is crucial to build resilience to environmental challenges. This involves preparing for and adapting to climate change impacts, such as extreme weather events and resource scarcity. Investing in disaster preparedness (my dad used to say saving for the rainy day), building climate-resilient infrastructure, and diversifying income sources can help mitigate the adverse effects of environmental shocks and protect against relapse into poverty.

Overcoming poverty requires a holistic approach that integrates environmental awareness and action. By understanding the environmental dimensions of poverty and taking proactive steps to address them, you can break free from the cycle of deprivation and create a more sustainable and prosperous future for yourself and your community. As stewards of the Earth, let us harness the power of environmental consciousness to pave the way towards a brighter tomorrow.

Chapter 10: The Journey to Financial Freedom: Empowering Yourself for Economic Independence

In this transformative chapter, we embark on our journey towards financial freedom a journey marked by self-discovery, empowerment, and the pursuit of economic independence. As we reflect on the insights gained throughout this book, we delve into actionable strategies and empowering mindset shifts that will empower readers to take control of their financial destinies and break free from the shackles of poverty.

Empowering Mindset Shifts:

The journey to financial freedom begins with a shift in mindset—a recognition that wealth is not solely determined by external circumstances, but also by our beliefs, attitudes, and actions towards money. By embracing a mindset of abundance, cultivating gratitude for what we have, and reframing our relationship with money, we can lay the foundation for lasting prosperity.

Setting Clear Financial Goals:

Central to achieving financial freedom is setting clear, achievable goals that align with our values, aspirations, and priorities. Whether it is saving for emergencies, paying off debt, or investing for the future, defining our financial goals provides a roadmap for success and empowers us to make intentional decisions that propel us towards our desired outcomes.

Developing Financial Literacy:

Empowering ourselves for economic independence also requires developing financial literacy—the knowledge and skills needed to make informed financial decisions. From understanding basic budgeting principles to navigating complex investment options, financial literacy equips us with the tools we need to build wealth, manage risk, and secure our financial futures.

Creating Multiple Streams of Income:

Do not forget the popular saying "jack of all trade master of none!" but in today's rapidly changing economy, diversifying income sources is key to achieving financial resilience and security. By exploring opportunities for additional income streams, such as starting a side hustle, freelancing, or investing in passive income-generating assets, readers can increase their earning potential and create a more stable financial foundation.

Building Wealth through Smart Investing:

Investing is a powerful tool for building wealth and achieving long-term financial goals. Whether it is investing in stocks, real estate, or retirement accounts, readers can harness the power of compounding returns to grow their wealth over time. By adopting a disciplined approach to investing, staying informed about market trends, and seeking professional advice when needed, readers can maximize their investment returns and accelerate their journey to financial freedom.

In our exploration of the journey to financial freedom, let us remember that true wealth is not measured solely by the size of our bank accounts, but by our ability to live life on our own terms, pursue our passions, and make a positive impact in the world. By embracing empowering mindset shifts, setting clear financial goals, developing financial literacy, creating multiple streams of income, and investing wisely, readers can empower themselves for economic independence and embark on a journey towards a life of abundance, fulfilment, and financial security.

Chapter 11: Final Reflections

In the concluding chapter of "Why are You Broke: Unravelling the Mysteries of Financial Struggle?", we find ourselves at the culmination of a profound journey, a journey of introspection, enlightenment, and empowerment. Throughout this book, we have delved deep into the complexities of poverty, exploring its myriad causes and consequences while uncovering insights and strategies for overcoming its grip.

I began this book with a statement from Jimmy Dean, an American actor, singer, and businessman, who came from a humble background. He was born into a financially struggling family in rural Texas in 1928. Growing up, Dean experienced poverty and worked various odd jobs to help support his family. Despite his challenging beginnings, Dean went on to achieve immense success in his career, becoming a renowned actor and country music artist, as well as a successful entrepreneur with ventures in the food industry.

His life story serves as an inspiration of overcoming adversity and achieving success through determination and hard work.

As we reflect on the insights gained from each chapter, we are reminded that poverty is not simply a matter of financial scarcity, but a complex web of social, economic, and environmental factors that intersect and intertwine in profound ways. From the structural inequalities that perpetuate cycles of deprivation to the systemic barriers that hinder upward mobility, we have confronted the harsh realities of poverty head-on, seeking to understand its roots and chart a path towards a more just and equitable society.

But amidst the challenges, we have also discovered glimmers of hope—stories of resilience, resourcefulness, and triumph against the odds. From the self-made entrepreneurs who rose from humble beginnings to the communities rallying together to protect and preserve their natural resources, we have witnessed the power of human agency and collective action to effect positive change in the face of adversity.

As we bid farewell to these pages, let us carry forward the lessons learned and the insights gained, knowing that the journey towards a world free from poverty is far from over. Let us continue to challenge injustice, advocate for equity, and strive towards a future where every individual could thrive and succeed, regardless of their background or circumstances.

And so, as we turn the final page of "Why are You Broke: Unravelling the Mysteries of Financial Struggle?", let us do so with a renewed sense of purpose and determination, knowing that together, we can build a brighter, more inclusive future for ourselves and generations to come.

www.ingramcontent.com/pod-product-compliance
Lightning Source LLC
Chambersburg PA
CBHW070414230526
45471CB00006B/2799